Burnt Toast

By
Kit Birks

MAPLE
PUBLISHERS

Burnt Toast

Author: Kit Birks

Copyright © 2025 Kit Birks

The right of Kit Birks to be identified as author of this work has been asserted by the author in accordance with section 77 and 78 of the Copyright, Designs and Patents Act 1988.

ISBN 978-1-83538-615-6 (Paperback)
978-1-83538-616-3 (E-Book)

Cover Design and Book Layout by:
Maple Publishers
www.maplepublishers.com

Published by:
Maple Publishers
Fairbourne Drive, Atterbury,
Milton Keynes,
MK10 9RG, UK
www.maplepublishers.com

A CIP catalogue record for this title is available from the British Library.

All rights reserved. No part of this book may be reproduced or translated by any form or by any means, electronic or mechanical, including photocopying, recording or by any information storage and retrieval system without written permission from the author.

The views expressed in this work are solely those of the author and do not necessarily reflect the views of the publisher, and the publisher hereby disclaims any responsibility for them.

This book is dedicated to my Mother, Father, Harry, Emily and Char,

For their love and patience through many years of pain,

Thank you for never leaving my side,

I love you all.

Contents

HURTING..05
Poems that reflect pain, struggle, and vulnerability

BLOOMING 29
Poems that explore healing, growth, and resilience

LOVING..53
Poems that express intimacy, connection, and love in all forms

OBSERVING..77
Poems reflecting on the beauty, complexity, and simplicity of life and nature

BECOMING..95
Poems that delve into self-discovery, transformation, and the journey of life

POEMS I WASN'T GOING TO INCLUDE 115
Poems I wasn't going to include but thought I'd see how others felt about them.

hurting

Burnt Toast

Lay me down and soak me in honey,
Let the sweetness take from me the bitter taste of pain,
Cover me entirely,
Immerse all my senses,
I don't want to see,
Or hear,
Or feel,
These dark memories again.

The weather keeps changing in my mind,
And just like the weather that surrounds me –
It's something I can't control,
I can try and make predictions,
Cross my fingers tightly that this massive storm will pass,
And the sunbeams will come piercing through the clouds,
Like little signals of hope for better things to come,
But maybe the problem is that I'm just sat,
Waiting for the storm to blow away,
What if I wrapped up and played with the wind,
Took my shoes off and danced in the rain,
Or if that was too much,
Sometimes used an umbrella for protection.

Because although this storm in my mind is going on right now,
If I can brave it,
And find my own sunbeams of hope,
Maybe the wait for a sunny day won't seem so far away.

I wonder if the ghosts like me,
Do they see what others don't,
Like how I tell my darkest secrets to dogs,
Or personify nature to feel less alone.

Do they see my ego blankets insecurity,
That my anger is from a place of pain,
That I struggle to live in the present,
Because of my past,
And I fear my future will be the same.

Do they see me?
Do they understand?
Do they forgive me?
The way I wish the living would.

Kit Birks

What is the point?
Of getting up when your body aches,
when the weight of the day feels heavier
than the bed you're lying in?
Of opening the curtains
when the world outside seems so indifferent?
Of putting one foot in front of the other
when you've already walked this road
and it led nowhere?

What is the point of trying
when failure feels inevitable?
Of speaking
when it feels like no one hears?
Of loving
when loss lingers in every corner of your heart?
What is the point
of holding on to something
that keeps slipping away?

I asked myself these questions.
I let them echo in the silence,
sit heavy in my chest,
pull me under more days than I can count,
And when the answers didn't come,
I stopped asking.
In fact,
I just stopped.

But even in the stopping,
life kept going.
The sun rose without my permission,
its light crawling across the floor
as if daring me to look.
The world kept spinning,

pulling me along with it,
even when I thought I couldn't move.

And somewhere in the haze,
there was a moment—
so small I almost missed it.
The gentle hug of a friend,
The sound of rain against the window,
soft and steady,
like it was washing something clean.
A memory of laughter,
how it felt in my chest
before the weight settled in.

So I got up,
not because I had answers,
but because staying down
felt like giving up on a question
I hadn't fully asked.

I started to notice the things
that hadn't left me:
the breath in my lungs,
the heartbeat that hadn't quit,
the way the sky changed colour every evening
as if it were trying to remind me
of something important.

And then, one day,
I found it again—
a moment where it all made sense.
Not everything, but enough.
Enough to see the beauty in the mess,
the meaning in the struggle,
the quiet resilience I hadn't realised
was mine all along.

Kit Birks

What is the point?
The point is this:
I got up,
and I'm glad I did.
I kept going,
and I'm grateful I tried.
I stood in the face of it all,
and I'm still here.

I'm alive,
and that is the point.

Burnt Toast

I watched her that day,
Her voice a blade cutting away,
'You're disgusting' she snapped, with ice in her tone,
'Do you think anyone loves you?"
No, you deserve to be alone".

'Stupid' she snapped at this girl's smallest mistake,
"You're a fool with no purpose, a life you forsake"
Her words lashed out, each one a sting,
"Every dream you touch means nothing?'.

She mocked her tears as they silently fell,
Called her worthless, a failure, a shell,
"you're not enough" she endlessly said.
Filling the silence with doubts she has bred.

No Kindness, no pause, just venom and shame,
A storm unleashed, a torrent of shame,
Her target stood frozen, just absorbing it all,
Shrinking smaller with each bitter call.

I stood there stunned as her cruelty unfurled,
A daggers edge aimed at this girl,
How could someone wield words so unkind,
So blind to the scars they were leaving behind.

But as I watched the truth became clearer,
Her target was actually trapped in a mirror,
There was no one else in that shadowed space,
Only her reflection, her own weary face.

Her voice cracked; her anger waned.
And the girl in the glass looked equally pained,
At war with herself, no truce in sight,
A battle she fought each day and each night.

Kit Birks

The mirror stared back, a silent plea,
For compassion, for softness to set her free,
she then reached for the glass with a trembling hand,
As if asking herself to understand.

"You're not perfect' she whispered, soft and low,
"But you're worthy of love, this I want you to know'.
The venom receded, the storm gave way,
To a fragile light that begged her to stay.

So let this be a lesson we hold,
A warning, a story worth being retold,
That the cruellest words we ever speak,
Are often to ourselves when we're feeling weak.

But healing begins when kindness takes hold,
When the word we speak are gentle and bold,
So, speak softly dear soul - with love and with grace,
The mirror deserves a kinder face.

Burnt Toast

Can you lie with me,
On our friend the grass,
So we can feel lost together.

Some days, I wish I owned a bakery,
Kneaded dough with my hands,
Made things,
Baked things,
Filled the air with sweetness,
Sweetness that will draw people in,
And they'll stop and say –
'Wow, that looks good',
Or,
'You made all this yourself?',
And I'll say, 'All in a day's work',
As I package their freshly made bread and slices of cake into small brown paper bags,
Their eyes full of happiness,
Already picturing the moment they're home with a cup of tea to enjoy it all.

Maybe what I want is to make people smile,
Or maybe,
Some days, I wish my efforts could be seen this easily,
That getting out of bed could be celebrated like carrot cake,
Brushing my teeth admired like cinnamon swirls,
That asking for help could be digested like choux buns.

Maybe it would be if I let people in,
Maybe it would be if I allowed others to help peel the blue from my skin.

Burnt Toast

Two wolves inside, they claw, they fight,
One feeds on darkness, the other on light,
The first a shadow, Born of rage and pain,
Its teeth sharp with hatred, Its howl fear untamed,
It thrives off self-destruction – on whispers of despair,
A beast of endless hunger, Pulling you to where –
The bottle, the powder, the needle, the flame,
Promise fleeting solace, then bury you in shame.

The other wolf is quieter, Its voice a gentle hum,
It waits beyond the chaos, for when the storm is done,
It speaks in words of kindness, a hope that softly glows,
A speck in the darkness, a path the weary know,
But its light feels faint, so distant and small,
When the shadow wolf is louder, Standing ten feet tall.

The darkness drew me closer, its voice a siren song,
It told me I was nothing and I couldn't last for long,
So I followed it down streets where the shadows loom tall,
Where the sun never rises, where the lost always crawl,
I traded my reflection for a mask that fit the part,
Played the role of the hollow, with an aching fractured heart,
Echoes in the hallway, whispers in my brain,
Promises of freedom, laced with whips of pain.

The demon wears a smile, a silver-tongued disguise,
A dealer of sweet nothings, spinning webs of lies,
I tried to drown it out, that gnawing in my chest,
But it grew with every swallow, with every stolen breath.
'I own you' it hissed, 'you're nothing without me',
So, I danced to its rhythm, thinking I was free.

Kit Birks

But freedom's a mirage, when you're shackled to the night,
With a hand around your throat, choking out the light,
But in the quiet moments, before the hunger screams,
A tiny voice within me, whispered forgotten dreams –
'Remember who you were before the poison kissed your lips,
Before the numbness settled, and your soul began to slip,
'Remember the laughter, the mornings soft and gold,
Before the cold consumed you before the lies took hold'.

So, the wolves began to battle, their roars tore through my chest,
Their claws scraped at my insides, refusing me my rest,
The darkness surged relentless, its fury sharp and wild,
But the light stood firm against it, unyielding, undefiled,
The shadow wolf would snarl, 'give up you'll never win',
While the other whispered softly, 'you can rise again'.

I lay there in the wreckage, caught between their rage,
A prisoner of my choices, locked inside this cage,
But somewhere in the silence, a new truth came alive,
That the war is never over, but you can choose which side survives.

I screamed into the void, 'take everything you've got',
'But you will never break me, no I won't be forgot',
The demon staggered backward, the chains began to slip,
I felt the weight of countless nights release its icy grip,
And though the wolves still circle, their eyes as black as sin,
The light inside me strengthens when I dare to let it in.

Now I walk this road, raw and battle worn,
Scars like constellations, a map where I was torn,
Two wolves still inside me, but now I hold the chain,
A testament to rising from the ashes of my pain,
I share my story with others, who are lost within the storm,
Who've traded dreams for chaos, left their hearts behind for harm,
Because although the darkness lingers, there's a power in the fight,
To wake each dare and whisper – 'not today, I choose the light'.

And what's in your rucksack?
Everything you need for the day,
A sandwich wrapped in tinfoil,
A coffee flask,
A notepad full of forgotten reminders,
And some extra change,
Maybe a mason jar of honey from that market back in town,
Something kind and extra-sweet to help get your feet back on the ground.

Too many floating thoughts about half lived realities,
Half smoked dreams,
Half smoked pack of cigarettes – would you share one with me?
I'll give you some thread in return so you can fix your broken seams,
That are bursting from the outdated versions of yourself,
Broken pieces of past,
You can't help but carry.

Maybe you don't mind the back ache,
Maybe you don't mind the cuts the straps make.

And isn't it funny how we all carry these rucksacks of life,
I wonder if you'd judge me if you looked into mine,
Maybe you'd help take a load off,
Or maybe you'd just add to it,
Maybe I need a mason jar of honey too,
I wonder if that mason jar of honey is you.

Sometimes all I want is to be held,
To use their arms like bubble wrap,
I want my cries to be muffled by the cotton of their T-shirt,
For my tears to run down skin that isn't mine,
To be wiped away by a hand that hasn't touched my pain.
I want my screaming heart to fall upon the ears of their understanding chest,
For the weight of my past to be held between their shoulders,
If only for a moment it could feel like a feather,
I want my thoughts to find peace within their presence,
For my aching bones to sigh into the cushion of their embrace,
As my tired eyes surrender to the duvet of their safety.

All I want is to be held,
For a little while,
For a long while,
For as long as I need.

Burnt Toast

Yesterday I was 8 years old,
and I did not worry about tomorrow,
I just went and played outside,
And it didn't matter if it was raining or if there was sunshine,
I did not care about the mud on my jeans,
Or the grass stains on my favourite t-shirt,
Because as if by magic they would always come back to me clean,
And I didn't think about what would happen if a thorn got caught under my skin,
Or if falling from a tree might make me bleed as a consequence,
But if it did,
I would just cry and run back inside,
And mum or dad would tell me that I will be alright,
As they lifted me onto the kitchen counter,
And cleaned the blood and the grit,
Before applying a plaster that had cartoon dinosaurs,
or space aliens on it,
And they'd say that they were proud of me,
For being so brave,
And they'd make me feel like it was okay to make mistakes.

And I can't tell you how two whole decades have passed since yesterday,
But suddenly I'm 28 and I cried today,
As I worried about tomorrow,
As I stayed inside to avoid the heavy rain,
And the things that might hurt me,
As I tried to get the stains out my clothes,
Yet they did not fade,
Just like all my mistakes,
As I lifted myself onto the kitchen counter,
And put a beige plaster on my cut,
And tried to make myself believe that I will be alright,
And that even though so much has changed since yesterday,
I must remember to still be proud of myself,
For being so brave.

Kit Birks

In my dream we are washing dishes,
Something simple, an afterthought of the day,
Your hands are there brushing against mine as you pass a plate,
I turn to catch you studying my side profile,
Our eyes linger, we share a smile,
A moment where seconds stretch to cradle our closeness,
The air around us is soft, gentle,
Like sunlight on closed eyes,
I can feel your presence in the spaces between us,
In the quiet breathes we share.

We move in silence but it's a silence rich,
Full of unspoken words, of things felt rather than said,
The kind of silence that speaks comfort,
Where the everyday becomes luminous.

There's nothing extraordinary here,
Just the rustling of cloth, the clinking of plates, the trickling of water,
But it feels sacred.
And I know, in the way dreams allow - that our love lives here,
The kind that breathes, wordless, steady as warm water.

But then the edges of the dream blur,
And I start to realise that I'm holding on too tight,
Trying to pull you with me, clinging to your presence,
As if I can keep it from fading.

But I feel myself slip away,
Falling back to the waking world,
Where the air is colder, empty, hollow,
Where the comfort of you is gone,
Leaving only the ache of your absence.

Burnt Toast

I reach out instinctively to the space where you should be,
But my hand only finds the t-shirt you left behind,
Folded on that chair - threadbare and worn,
I clutch it to my chest,
The last remnants of your warmth, soft as memory.
And somehow, even in the emptiness I feel you,
Your safety woven into the cotton,
As if the fabric remembers what it was like to hold you close.

To those of you that are living half dead,
Feeling as empty as the bottles bedside of your bed,
Filling them back up just to drain them again,
Because facing reality brings nothing but dread,
It's okay,
I get it,
I've been there too my friend,
Chewing the same page of the same chapter over and over again,
Repetitive cycle,
Same start,
Same end.

You chew and you chew,
Until its stuck like a seed (you know when one gets tightly wedged in your teeth),
But what if I gave you a pen,
A blank sheet,
And told you today doesn't have to be a repeat,
You can rewrite the page, the chapter, in fact a whole book,
Rediscover yourself,
A new you,
A new look,
Because this character you're playing is only headed one way,
An untimely death,
A life of blacked out days.

But I promise you if you're willing to change,
My hands are open for you to spit out the page,
It will be uncomfortable,
Your mouth it might bleed,
But things will get better,
Just wait and you'll see,

Burnt Toast

That you have the power to rewrite your story,
To one filled with hope,
Facing the addict within,
One where you recover,
One where you live.

Kit Birks

I'm standing on the edge where the air feels like glass,
A brittle silence that shatters the past,
A breath caught in my throat, a scream trapped in my chest,
Each second a question, no answer, no rest.

The void looks peaceful, it beckons, it sways,
A hypnotic rhythm that pulls me away.
"Come closer," it whispers, "just one small step,
The pain will dissolve, and you'll finally forget."

I've fought this voice before, its honeyed deceit,
It wraps around my ankles, tangles my feet,
It tells me I'm nothing, a shadow, a stain,
That my absence would wash away everyone's pain.

I nod along, though I know it's a lie,
Still, the logic feels clearer the more that I try.
"You're a burden," it says, "they'll all be free—
The world will keep spinning, just fine without me."

The edge feels closer, the pull feels strong,
Like I've been marching toward it my whole life long.
And maybe I have-every scar, every tear,
Has carved out this path to this place of despair.

But in the dark, there's a glint of light,
A voice I can barely hear through the night.
It's small, it's broken, but steady and true,
And it whispers, "Stay. There's more for you."

I shake my head; I don't want to believe,
But the voice grows louder, refusing to leave.
It reminds me of laughter, of mornings and rain,
Of hands that held mine through the thickest of pain.

Burnt Toast

"You've fought this before," the voice softly pleads,
"And each time you've planted unshakable seeds.
The edge isn't freedom; it's the thief of your name,
And you're more than this sorrow, more than this shame."

I falter, I stumble, tears blur my sight,
The edge feels so close, but the voice burns bright.
It speaks of a sunrise I've yet to see,
Of love I can give, of who I could be.

I take a step back, trembling, unsure,
But the voice holds steady, quiet and pure.
"Not today," it says, "not now, not tonight-
The battle's not over; stay in the fight."

The edge doesn't vanish, it lingers and hums,
A reminder of the battles I've fought and I've won.
The void may call, but I'll answer with breath-
One small defiance in the face of death.

I'll stumble, I'll falter, I'll ache, I'll cry,
But I'll cling to the light and give life one more try,
Because the edge isn't the end— it's just one place,
And there's more to this journey, more steps, more space.

So, I pull myself from the dark, leave the edge behind,
Turn from the chaos and seek peace of mind.
I'm still here, still breathing, still fighting, still whole—
A battle-scarred heart, but an unbroken soul.

Kit Birks

I put bread in the toaster and all I get is burnt toast,
I put milk in my coffee and my mug overflows,
I get dressed and put jeans on but they're on the wrong way round,
I've missed a button on my shirt and find my socks have holes in the toes.

So I go back to bed,
Touch nothing for the rest of the day,
Because it seems as though my hands have turned into grenades,
But then my stomach starts rumbling,
And my mouth feels dry,
My bare skin is covered in goosebumps,
And my mind is feeding me lies.

I keep staring at my hands
And staring at my skin,
And staring at my life,
And wondering where do I begin?

Keep touching nothing,
Doing nothing,
Being nothing,
Or try again?

Because everyone burns toast.

Kit Birks

blooming

Burnt Toast

She did not declare her arrival,
Tiptoeing into my bed late at night
So quiet she did not wake me,
Yet her gentle presence was shifting my unconscious mind,
Turning my nightmares into dreams,
And calming my restless movements and thoughts.
She held me when I woke,
And the comfort of her powerful silence,
Deafened my racing mind,
Her embrace so familiar it's like she had never left.

I wanted to be angry,
She had left me alone for so long,
But how could I be,
When she was here to save me.

So with eyes wide open,
And a life waiting beyond my duvet,
I took her hand and welcomed her back into my life.

Hope.

I went to watch the sunrise
I hoped my troubled mind would vanish with the night,
So, I drove,
And I sat,
And I waited for the sunlight,
But as it came so did my disappointment.

There was no tapestry of colour,
The rays didn't stretch across the sky,
The light was patchy and dull,
The selfish clouds hid the awaited beauty from my eyes,
The darkness had only shift from black to grey,
So, my worries were not taken from me but rather stayed.

So, Frustrated,
I stood,
And I walked,
And I realised,
That the sun has good days,
And bad days,
And yesterdays,
But every day,
She wakes up and does her best to shine.

Burnt Toast

I'm sorry dying didn't work out for you.
Quite funny, really—
You did it because you were failing at life,
and then, well …. you failed at death too.

Guess you're stuck here now.
Poor you.
Poor, dear, unlucky you,
With your whole messy life stretched out ahead,
Like a novel too boring to finish.
Another day, another sigh, another hour wondering why -
You'll have to get up, you'll have to move.
You'll have to stumble into the unforgiving groove
of this so-called life.

Get dressed, brush your teeth.
Drag your weary limbs to the shop for bread you might not even eat.
And don't forget the milk—
Because the cat's not giving up on you just yet.

You'll have to open the fridge and sigh at its emptiness.
You'll have to answer a text you're too tired to read,
or hear a phone ring that you'd rather ignore.
Another bill to pay, another floor to clean.
Another hour to fill with absolutely nothing in between.

But here's the thing no one tells you,
The thing that's always been true:
By being bad at dying,
You have a second shot at living.

Kit Birks

And so, like a bad movie with a surprisingly good second act,
One day, you'll stand by a window and realize the sunlight looks new.
You'll crack it open and feel the breeze sigh on your face,
Like it missed you, like the world missed you.

You'll hear birds singing louder than your fears,
their little wings flapping through the years
you thought you'd never survive.
You'll stand outside, alive.
Really alive,
And slowly, the cracks in your armour will begin to shine.
Failure might've brought you here, "but this life…",
You'll whisper, "It's still mine."

You'll feel it in the laughter of strangers,
In the rhythm of waves,
In that split-second look that someone gave—
The one that says, 'Don't go just yet.'

Because the truth is,
You're about to see sunsets that melt the sky in gold.
You're about to love stories that beg to be told.
You'll cry over movies, dance in the rain,
Let joy slip into your body again.

You get to learn what it feels like,
When someone holds you as if you're made of stars.
Start to see you're enough,
Just as you are.

You'll hear a song and hum along,
Find strength where you thought you were only weak.
One day, you'll notice your heart speaks—
And this time, you'll actually listen.

Burnt Toast

You'll sip coffee that tastes like a poem.
You'll laugh so hard ,
You'll think, 'this must be home',
And you'll wonder, quietly, how you ever believed,
that the end was the best you could achieve.

So yeah, I'm sorry dying didn't work out for you.
But honestly? One day you'll see,
That a failure is sometimes the best thing you can be.

Kit Birks

Happiness is not dead,
It's not lost forever,
It's there,
Waiting to be found.

It's kiss me quick before they see,
It's being on the verge of losing hope and having an epiphany,
Its revelry,
Its lying with the one you love in ecstasy,
'You and me',
You say that's all we need.

It's that book beside your bed with hundreds of dog-eared pages,
It's your favourite song,
Your favourite cake,
Only the recipe always changes –
Unmeasured and untimed but always baked to perfection.

It's light, Its laughter,
It's before's, it's afters,
It's that moment it our day that allows us to breathe,
Takes our worries away.

Its church windows singing to their God up above,
Its faith and belief,
Its sweet honey and love,
It's the answers to our prayers,
It's being you without a care,
It doubles when its shared,
It's a smile after months of despair,
So, I promise its always there.

Burnt Toast

Happiness – its lives inside us all,
It lives inside you,
Inside me,
We just can't always predict when,
Or what,
Might set it free.

Kit Birks

Don't just show me the best parts of you,
I'm not scared of the dark,
I'm a visitor there too.

Burnt Toast

Your body is yawning,
Your fingertips are weary from picking up your fragmented sense of self,
Let me take the pieces,
I'll wrap them in cotton wool to keep them safe.

Then you can rest darling one,
Let the slumber in your eyes drift into your mind,
Let the demons fall from your thoughts onto your pillow,
And escape down your duvet.

You'll soon wake to the sound of sunshine,
Where we can put you back together again,
Using pieces of gold,
So, you can show the world how you fell apart,
Only to come back more beautiful than you were before.

Don't hold it in,
Be a hot, sexy, vulnerable mess and cry in front of me.

Burnt Toast

When summer is over,
Autumn comes to call,
Green leaves change their colour,
Before they start to fall.

Bare branches are then left swinging,
Facing wind, rain and snow,
Nothing to protect them-
On the floor their old brown coat,
Which is sinking into the soil,
Feeding the roots below,
This energy is needed,
To help the new leaves grow.

So when you feel cold and broken,
Vulnerable and exposed,
Trust the process that's unfolding,
The wintering is part of growth.

There's a fork in my drawer
that doesn't match the others.
A Tupperware lid with no container.
A single sock, balled up in defiance.

They don't complain.
They're not bitter.
They've accepted their freedom.
A fork can still poke at pancakes.
A lid can hold keys or loose change.
A sock makes a great hand puppet
or a dusting mitt in a pinch.

We call them "lost,"
but what if they're just beginning?
Breaking free of expectations,
shaking off the rules of "sets" and "pairs."

And what if we, too,
could embrace being a little unmatched?
A little misplaced?
A little free?

Not everything has to belong to something else.
Sometimes, it's enough
just to belong to yourself.

Burnt Toast

Step with me as we breathe in the sadness,
Step with me as we breathe it out again.

Kit Birks

You know that moment when you get caught under a big wave,
It spins you round and around,
You start forgetting which way is the surface and which is the ocean floor,
So, you swim into the direction you think is up,
But your nose grazes the sand,
You try again,
But the motion of the water is still twisting and turning you,
So again, your nose bumps into the ocean floor.

This can continue for what feels like a lifetime,
The panic sets in,
Your brain doesn't communicate with your body,
And all you can think is –
'I must get to the surface',
'I must get to the surface'.

And then it happens,
Your face pushes past water into the air,
You grab at the air taking a breath,
Your hands come towards your eyes to remove the salt water,
You take a moment –
You let the relief rush over,
And before long you start swimming again.

To me,
This is the process of healing,
The wave which once consumed you will settle,
And you will find your way back to the surface again.
You will swim above the moments,
That so nearly sunk you.

Let's open a bottle of our finest emotions,
And get drunk on vulnerability.

Dear Death,
I've been meaning to get in contact,
But the days they slip away,
'I think about you often',
I wonder if that's what you're expecting me to say,
I know we had an understanding, and I thought I'd made up my mind,
You lingered like a lover, waiting patient, gentle, kind,
For a while I felt your comfort, the pull of letting go,
But there's something I need to tell you, something you deserve to know.

See, I thought I was ready, ready to fall into your arms,
You'd take away the pain, the weight, you'd quiet all my storms,
But you wouldn't bring me joy Death, no light, no second chance,
You'd leave me empty, motionless, no more opportunities to dance,
And I thought that's what I wanted, for a while I believed it true,
But Life came knocking softly, a whisper in the blue.

She didn't shout or pull me back, no grand romantic scene,
Just reminded me it's okay to need help and that the pain doesn't mean I'm weak,
She pulled me from my static grave, out the duvet into day,
And showed me beauty's subtle truths, in mundane gentle ways,
She took my tears and traded them for sun-bleached skies and peace,
When night returned, she taught me even darkness has release.

Life reminded me she loves me, though I'd turned my back on her,
Her touch was warm, familiar, she said 'you still have so much more',
More time to heal, to learn, to see, more chances to begin,
More mornings filled with golden light that kiss my fragile skin.

Burnt Toast

I won't lie it wasn't easy, letting go of what we planned,
But Life held out her broken heart and I took it in my hands,
The flames I thought had vanished, were embers glowing low,
And with time and space I fed them, now they're burning,
Don't you know?

I even faced the ugly parts, every wound I used to hide,
The regret and wrong decisions, but it didn't mean I died,
Because healing isn't a pretty song, its blood, its grit, its fire,
Its learning strength can rise from cracks, not perfection or desire.

So, there's no doubt we'll be together again,
But I hope in many years time,
When grey hair is laced with experiences gained,
And wrinkles show my laughter lines,
So don't see this as rejection, I'll meet you there with open arms,
For now, I hope you understand that Life's the one that hold my heart.

So, Dear Death,
Sorry I left you waiting but I've got more love I need to start,
More moments to unravel, more Life to fill my heart,
How long for? I couldn't tell you,
I guess it's written in the stars,
But for now, Life is the lover I must cherish,
Until Death do us part.

She traded bars for coffee shops,
Cheap wine for a stable state of mind,
One-night highs for a real chance at life.

You see we've been brought up believing,
A good time is found in lager tops,
Tequila shots, late night corner shops and drunken thoughts,
That the only way to celebrate our achievement in life is by numbing our minds,
So, it should come as no surprise that for some,
A drunken haze, gets turned into drunken ways,
That continue for the rest of their drunken days,
Pints used as ammunition to create devastation,
Where happiness used to lie.

No longer raising a glass in celebration,
But to lost hope and commiseration,
Thinking the only way to get through is repeating the grind of constant intoxication,
Living a life through this obsessive manifestation,
It's no wonder us addicts feel like giving up on this life.

But, suddenly there comes a day,
A moment,
A flicker of light,
That hope is still out there,
If we can change our ways,
And leave our old selves behind.

It can seem impossible to face the rest of our lives,
Without any substances to alter our minds,
But the big picture doesn't have to be hung yet,
Just breathe,
And remember one day at a time.

Burnt Toast

Because soon you'll realise,
Looking at the world through sober eyes,
That the true highs in life,
Are the ones that have always been around you,
In lollipops, forehead kisses and candyfloss skies.

So, she traded bars for coffee shops,
Cheap wine for a stable state of mind,
One-night highs for a real chance at life – why?
It's the change she needed in order to survive,
To stay alive,
To truly start to thrive.

Kit Birks

There is sunshine pouring from your skin,
Whole worlds waiting beyond your ribcage,
A universe ready to escape with every word you utter,
And you say you aren't enough?

My darling,
You are quite simply,
Everything.

Burnt Toast

Be kinder.
Not just to others but also to yourself.
Be careful with your heart,
gentle with your mind,
and wise with your words.

Let your heart fall in love
with who you are—
the beauty, the scars,
the stories they hold.
Let your mind believe it,
with every breath,
with every thought that dares to doubt.

Speak to yourself as a friend,
soft and steady,
in the way you'd hope
others might speak to you—
lifting, not breaking,
healing, not harming.

Be kinder.
Because the world needs your light,
But so do you.

Kit Birks

Think of the million tiny things that had to fall into place to bring you here,
to this moment, right now.
Every fleeting choice, every step forward or back,
Every word spoken or swallowed,
Every glance, every quiet, unnoticed motion.

They gathered, linked together in a chain so fragile,
It's a wonder it didn't break.
And yet, here you are.

Here you are listening to this, wearing that, feeling this way.
Loving someone, missing someone, breaking, healing,
Laughing, aching, holding on, letting go, existing.

A million alternate outcomes hover in the shadows—
roads not taken, lives unlived, doors left closed,
choices that could have sent you spinning into another reality.

But this, THIS is the thread the universe chose for you.
This is the moment handed to you.
Not as a punishment, not as a prize, but as a question:
What will you do with this?

And I don't know if this moment feels heavy—
if your chest tightens under its weight,
if the sharp edges of life are cutting too deep.
Or if it feels light, like the soft glow of sunrise breaking through the night.

But know this: the next moment is still unwritten.
This is not the end,
It's a pause, a comma, a single brushstroke on the canvas,
a single stitch in the tapestry you are weaving,
Thread by thread, moment by moment, choice by choice.

Burnt Toast

And you may not see it now, may not feel its beauty yet, but it's there, taking shape.

Even the tangled knots, the frayed edges, the colours that seem out of place—
they are part of the picture,
And maybe, just maybe,
This picture will become your most breath-taking work yet.

So, hold this thread, this moment, this choice.
It's yours to shape, yours to carry.
And remember,
even now, a million tiny things
are conspiring to move you forward.

Let them.

Kit Birks

loving

Burnt Toast

How do you say goodnight to someone who's not near?
Do you reach at the sky, write a message in the stars,
Polish the moon, make it bright, so they're not alone in the dark,
Re-arrange the planets to create their favourite piece of art.

Maybe, speak sonnets at the wind and pray it will carry them clear,
Sing poetry to the trees loud enough to fill their ears,
Whisper over a million pillows in the hope that they will hear.

Or maybe really all you can do,
Is close your eyes and think of them,
Knowing you love them,
And they love you.

Kit Birks

I don't want the perfect house,
But one with different sized windows,
Rugs with threads loose at the edges,
And sofas scattered with mismatching pillows.

Where it's okay to forget to take off muddy shoes,
And dogs can sleep on all of the furniture,
Where the kitchen will show memories of cooking together,
With knife marks,
And coffee rings,
And sauce stains,
On different spots on the counters.

A place where the walls will breathe music,
And curtains will let in the sun,
Where the beds don't always have to be made,
So there's evidence of where we lay wrapped together as one.

It will match my scratches,
And cracks and faults,
It won't make me leave them by the front door,
So when your love comes knocking,
Please know,
You'll be welcomed in with every imperfection and flaw.

Burnt Toast

She wants an organic kind of love,
An heirloom tomato,
Purple sprouting broccoli,
Not wrapped in plastic kind of love.

A potato still covered in soil,
Leeks with grit between the layers,
Misshaped carrot,
Long-stemmed asparagus,
Take as much as you want,
Take as much as you need,
This was grown with time,
This was grown with care,
Kind of love.

A let this develop naturally,
Let this be unforced,
Let this not be perfect,
Kind of love.

A pick me because I'm worth it,
Pick me even though you see my flaws,
Pick me because you'll love me anyway,
Pick me because you know I'm tastier,
Kind of love.

Kit Birks

Maybe in another life we never even meet,
Maybe in another life we are sworn enemies,
Or the best of friends,
Maybe in another life you sell me flowers in the market,
And we chat about the weather as you put a bouquet of tulips together for me,
Maybe in another life you're the colleague that's always late,
And I'm the boss that you absolutely hate,
Maybe in another life you're an annoying neighbour,
Who is always noisy and puts rubbish in my bin,
Maybe in another life our eyes cross at the bar,
And we find each other good looking but we never even speak,
Maybe in another life we simply brush past each other in the street.

Maybe in another life we do end up together,
And we don't give up,
And we make it work,
And we get to love each other forever,
And we get to make memories,
And have children,
And create a home,
We get to kiss each other goodbye every morning,
And spend evenings talking about our days,
We get to plan adventures and go on holidays,
And spend car rides singing our favourite songs,
We get to hold each other when life gets tough,
And we get to see our laughter lines grow deeper and deeper,
As the years pass.

But in this life,
We are just a chapter in one another's book,
And even though we don't want that to end,
Maybe this is how it's meant to be,
Because in this life we are just a stepping stone for each other,
In order to find a forever kind of love,
One that doesn't hold the weight of all these maybes.

Burnt Toast

I loved you like the sun loves the horizon—
aching, reaching, never quite touching,
but always burning for the moment
our worlds would collide.

You were every "what if" I ever dared to dream,
every soft breath against my neck
on the nights the world felt too loud
and I needed silence that spoke.

But love is a cruel teacher, isn't it?
It hands you everything,
then asks if you're brave enough
to lose it.
I wasn't ready for the way your absence
would echo—
like an empty room where laughter once lived,
like a song I forgot how to sing
but still hum under my breath.

And yet—
even in the leaving, even in the breaking,
there was beauty.
Because love doesn't vanish; it transforms.
It becomes the way I still look for you
in sunsets and strangers,
the way I smile when I hear your name,
even if my chest tightens too.

If you were a lesson,
then I have learned this:
to love someone is to give them the power
to shatter you,
and to let them go
is to gather the pieces
and rebuild yourself stronger.

I loved you,
and I still do—
not in the way of holding on,
but in the way of releasing,
letting the wind carry you
to wherever you need to be.

And maybe that's what love truly is—
not the staying,
not the keeping,
but the letting go,
with hands that tremble
and a heart that still whispers,
"Thank you for everything."

Burnt Toast

Imagine a world where no one hides.
Where the trembling voice that says, "I'm not okay",
Is met with an echo of kindness,
Not silence, not shame.
Where every tear is caught, not questioned.

Here, the mind is not a battleground,
but a garden.
Every scar, every shadow tended with care,
Soft hands pulling weeds while planting seeds of hope.

No one says, "Be stronger,"
Because strength is redefined—
It's in the asking, the sharing,
The showing up when it hurts the most.

In this place loneliness finds no home.
Every locked door is met with a knock,
Every "I'm fine" met with, "Tell me more."

Imagine doctors prescribing sunlight and rest,
A friend delivering flowers to celebrate the day, you asked for help.
Imagine a stranger on the train offering you their seat—
Not for your body, but for your tired soul.

Imagine schools teaching empathy like arithmetic—
How to divide burdens,
How to multiply joy.
Imagine workplaces with quiet rooms,
Midday pauses for deep breaths,
Managers who ask, "Are you thriving?"
and mean it.

Kit Birks

Here, the nights don't feel endless.
Someone always answers the phone,
Always sits beside you,
Until your silence softens into words.
You aren't "broken" for feeling deeply,
For needing time, for being human.

And there are no masks,
No forced smiles or hidden tears.
Every face is honest,
Every struggle seen as a thread in the fabric we all share.

When you fall, no one looks away.
They reach down, not to save you,
But to stand with you until you're ready to rise.

In this world, pain is not a weakness,
But a passage.
And love isn't rare—
It's the air we breathe,
The language we speak,
The ground we walk upon together.

Burnt Toast

Curl me up and put me in your shirt pocket,
Let me sway as you breathe,
Let me sleep to your heartbeat,
Let me stay,
So, I can be with you everywhere you go.

Kit Birks

I've been thinking a lot lately about love—the kind you find in books and movies,
The kind that sweeps you off your feet, that makes you believe in something bigger than yourself. I know it's idealistic, and maybe a little romanticised, but there's something in those stories that just speaks to me.

In books and movies, love feels like magic. It's not perfect, and it doesn't come without its challenges, but it's deep and true. The characters face impossible odds, yet somehow, they always find their way back to each other. There's this sense of destiny, of two people being meant for one another in a way that makes everything else fade into the background. I guess that's what I want—to find a love that feels like it was written just for me.

I want the kind of love that's not afraid to show its flaws, the kind that grows stronger through the struggles. The love that changes you in all the right ways, making you braver, kinder, and more yourself than you've ever been. I know life isn't a movie, and love doesn't always look like the stories we see on screen, but that doesn't stop me from hoping.

I want to believe in the kind of love that makes you feel seen and understood, the kind that can turn even the most ordinary moments into something beautiful. A love that feels like coming home after being lost for so long. Maybe it's rare, maybe it's messy and unpredictable, but it's out there.

I guess what I'm trying to say is that I don't want to settle for anything less than that kind of love. I'm holding out for the story that feels like it's been waiting for me all along—the one that brings all the pieces together in a way that finally makes sense.

Until then, I'll keep dreaming and keep believing that love like that exists. Somewhere.

Burnt Toast

The Garden in my heart had slowly started to die,
Lavender had become damp,
Roses had collected dust,
Tulips were moth eaten,
Stale were the buttercups.

Azaleas were musty,
Daises had grown mould,
Asters were layered in mildew,
Rotten were the marigolds.

Everything was weathered,
Wilted down,
Withered in pain,
There was a subdued hum of acceptance,
That nothing new would bloom again.

But you swept the dying petals,
The broken stems,
The dried-up leaves,
Scattered new seeds,
Blossoming,
The most beautiful garden my heart had seen.

You make me feel worthy of love,
Even on the days my soul isn't full of sunshine.

Burnt Toast

I don't know the name of the God you whisper to,
or if you bow to none at all,
but feel the weight of the stars
pressed into your palms at night.

Perhaps your god hums in the wind
that tangles through your hair,
or settle in the stillness of morning,
when the world holds its breath.
Maybe God is the ocean's pull,
or the laughter of someone who knows your name
like it was written in the first language.

Perhaps your god lives in the seeds
that break through stubborn earth,
or the way rain cleanses everything,
even the places we thought were beyond repair.

You might not call your God, 'God',
Maybe you call it hope.
Maybe it's the love in someone's eyes
when you think you deserve none.
Maybe you don't know yet,
and that's okay too.

What matters isn't the shape or the name,
but the way it softens the sharp edges of the world,
how it reminds you to keep breathing
when the air feels like glass.

Kit Birks

We find God in the spaces between—
in the stillness after a storm,
in the long embrace that softens grief,
in the hand that reaches for yours,
in the courage to get up
when everything inside you says, "Stay down."

What matters is what it does for you—
how it builds a bridge
when all you see is water,
how it threads a light
through the needle of your darkest days.

And whether you kneel or dance or cry,
whether you believe or just hope,
know this:
God is not far.
It is the pulse beneath your skin,
the fire in your chest,
the voice that says,
"You are more than what you've lost."

It is the road beneath your weary feet,
the whisper that calls you home
to yourself,
again, `and again.
And when you doubt,
it is the sun rising anyway,
a quiet reminder
that even in the absence of faith,
you are held.

Burnt Toast

You are the un-mouldy strawberry in an out-of-date punnet,
You are the one patch of shade on a hot summer's day,
You are the 50pence piece found when needed for parking,
You are the cloudless bit of sky in one that's otherwise full of rain.

You are the woolly jumper when the heating's not working,
You are the pen found when something needs to be written down,
You are the one pair of tights without any ladders,
You are the last seat left on a busy commuter train.

You are the second rainbow that no one saw coming,
You are the storm that holds off until I just get inside,
You are the matching pair of socks in a drawer full of odd ones,
You are the coat that perfectly covers the big coffee stain.

You are these twists of fate that make me feel lucky,
You are the little miracles that help me keep sane,
You are exactly what I need and all that I wanted,
You are the reasons I smile every single day.

Kit Birks

I don't want you to feel lonely,
Or sad,
Or lost,
Or like the thought of breathing is too much,
But if you do,
Please close your eyes and start to picture us.

We're lying under a willow tree,
With grass below,
And breeze above,
The bees are playing music,
And our hands are laced in knots.

So, see I'm always with you,
In presence,
Or in thought,
And without you here,
To love you dear,
I would feel lonely too.

When the world is sleeping,
There is darkness all around,
The trees aren't even sighing,
The whispering wind has settled down,
I close my eyes to join them,
In this place of rest,
Because it's there I get to see you,
The land of dreams,
Within my head.

Kit Birks

The next person I fall in love with—
please, don't be perfect.
I want to see your quirks, the ones you try to hide—
the way you tap your foot when you're thinking,
the weird hum that escapes when you're cooking,
the laugh that's a little too loud
and makes your eyes squint like you're in the sun.

Please,
leave your mistakes on the table,
your messy bits,
the ones that make you human
and real.
Tell me about the time you tried to fix something and only made it worse
or when you cried watching a rom-com and couldn't stop,
because you just really, really needed to.

I want to know what breaks you,
what makes you angry in the little, hilarious ways—
like when you stub your toe and curse in a way that makes me laugh
because it's not even a real swear word.
I want to see you trying to explain,
why you bought three house plants
and then forgot to water them
until they looked like sad, green spaghetti.

Show me your bad days,
the ones where you don't brush your hair
and you wear your oldest hoodie
that smells like home
and maybe a bit like coffee.
I want the mess of your mind—
the random thoughts you throw at me

Burnt Toast

like, "Do you think penguins get jealous?"
and then we'll talk about that for half an hour
because we've got nothing better to do.
I want the "oops" moments,
the ones that leave us both laughing
until we forget what we were even laughing about.

I'll love the version of you
who still hasn't figured out how to fold a fitted sheet
without swearing under your breath,
who spills something on their shirt
and then spends twenty minutes
trying to scrub it out
with a tiny napkin
like it's going to help.

Just Please,
don't be perfect.
I don't need flawless,
just real,
and I'll be here—
seeing every part of you,
the good, the bad,
and every weird, wonderful and messy thing in between.
Because perfect is boring.
But you?
You're a hot mess I could live in forever.

Kit Birks

My home doesn't have a door,
It doesn't have any windows,
It doesn't have any doors,
There is no place to hang a painting,
To boil a kettle,
Or store a coat.

There is no place to put your feet up,
To run a bath,
And have a soak.

But I promise you can live there,
In fact you already do,
My home is in my heart,
And I saved the best room for you.

Burnt Toast

We are made up of the people we've met,
the ones we've loved,
and those who've left their mark on us in ways we don't always realize.
Every person we've cared about has imprinted a piece of themselves onto us.,
It's in the small things—the recipe we still make because they showed us how,
the song that instantly takes us back to a moment shared,
the way we laugh or say a certain phrase because we picked it up from them.

Sometimes, we do things a certain way because an ex-lover did it like that,
and without thinking, it became part of our routine,
A friend's sense of humour might live on in our own,
or a stranger we once met may have introduced us to a passion that now defines us.
It's as if we carry all these fragments of people within us,
weaving them into the fabric of who we are.

We are not just our own experiences,
but a beautiful mosaic of others—friends, family, lovers,
even those who drifted away long ago,
their influences shape the way we see the world,
how we navigate it and how we express love, joy, and pain.

Each person has left their fingerprint on us,
and in that, we carry pieces of them forward.
It's beautiful to think that we are all living,
breathing collections of the connections we've made.
Even when people leave,
whether by choice or circumstance,
parts of them remain.
And in that way, we're never truly alone—
we are made up of love, memories, and the essence of every soul that's touched ours.

Burnt Toast

I like to think that at the beginning of time,
There were thousands of stars up in the sky,
And after a while they began to crash and collide,
Until these stars became dust,
That fell to the earth,
And eventually,
After different forms and rebirths,
This dust became people,
And people found love,
Gravitating towards each other,
A force that seemed sent from above.

So I think when I found you,
I wasn't only drawn to your shine,
But amongst life's dark chaos,
I found a missing part of my light,
Like somehow,
We were finally back intertwined.
It had found its way home,
Your stardust and mine.

Kit Birks

observing

My dear friend the breeze,
I see you,
Stroking the fresh coats of summer trees,
Their green leaves bouncing and you breathe onto them.

Transforming fields into rippling grassy seas,
The waves ridden by plump bees,
Now full, from lunching on wildflowers.

Your sighs hugging everything I see,
Your sighs hugging every part of me,
Me –
Just another piece of nature,
Just another piece of nature.

How lucky I am to have a friend like you,
My dear friend the breeze.

Kit Birks

The words of water whisper over the weeds,
Soft sentences flowing down stream,
Giving life to all that rests on the riverbed,
So quiet,
So calm,
So serene.

But if you stop,
Sit to watch,
The way it flits and floats,
And weaves over all that it sees,
You'll hear its gentle roar.

Soft giant,
So happy to be free,
Loving water please –
Will you teach me?

Burnt Toast

Its August - British "summertime",
Yet I'm sat in the rain, growing cold and frustrated after missing my train,
And to make things worse the next one is hugely delayed.
So I'm sat waiting for it to come,
On a damp bench that's making my bum numb,
Sipping an iced coffee (which is now a choice I rather regret),
But thinking you paid £3.80 for this so you're going to enjoy it nonetheless.

So I'm sipping,
And I'm waiting,
And I can't help but watch the little piece of world I now find myself a part of.

There's a couple who are trying to pull their coats over their heads,
But its not working,
So they're still getting absolutely drenched,
Which is making them laugh,
As one pulls the other closer to kiss them gently on the neck.

There's a little boy,
Playing with his dinosaur toy,
A toy which is clearly very well loved,
And he's making it ROAR whilst bounding it down a red brick wall,
Probably imagining a world where this small stuffed T-Rex is in fact 20ft tall.

On the platform across from me,
I see this cute scruffy terrier – shaking,
It must be soaked to the bone,
And his owner is bending down to put on this silly (but adorable) little raincoat,
Which doesn't seem to bother the pup one little bit,

Infact, he seems rather thankful,
Showing gratitude with tiny loving licks.

Next to me are two elderly men with matching white flat caps on,
Which makes me smile as it reminds me how a friend recently told me that he wanted one,
Anyway,
I can hear them nattering,
Little burbles of content,
Joking with each other as they agree that they 'scrub up well',
Adding 'we're not too bad for two old fellas'.

Standing in front of me there's a brave woman without a coat,
She turns and I see her t-shirt says, 'sober is sexy',
And I find myself smiling and nodding because I wholeheartedly agree,
And she catches my eye and smiles right back at me,

And I think Is this love?
Probably,
But just another that passes me by like when I am on the tube or on the bus.

So as my gaze lowers to my phone on my lap,
Which is flashing '1% battery left',
I think this could have been the straw that broke the camel's back,
But instead, I think aren't I lucky,
I'll have a whole train journey to just sit and soak myself in the small joys of living presently.

Burnt Toast

How can you be bored,
The world is art.

I went out for my morning run,
The sun hadn't risen yet,
But there was a gentle light helping me navigate my footsteps,
And I ran under a canopy of bare branches,
Stark silhouettes against the twilight,
And I remembered how I once dreamt of being a tree,
And I stood tall in a forest amongst my other tree friends,
And I drank sky and munched on sunlight,
Shared hugs through my branches and leaves,
Spoke through my roots about nutrients and water and insect news,
Became a home to birds, squirrels, moss and mushrooms,
Played with the wind,
Grew with the years,
Changed with the seasons,
No worries,
No stress,
I could just be a tree in blissful acceptance.

And now as I ran through winters air,
It looked like the trees were sleeping,
And I wondered if perhaps they were the ones now dreaming,
Perhaps dreaming about me,
About being human,
How we are free to walk and roam because we aren't planted in one place,
How we can uplift our roots and bring them with us,
Sink our feet into sand, mud, grass,
Sink our hearts into people, places, music, poetry, art,
That we get to cry and laugh,
Carry our homes with us filling it with all the things that make us feel complete,
That if we set our minds to it,
We can be anything we want to be.

Burnt Toast

So, I looked up to the trees and how no doubt they were living up to my dreams,
And I thanked them for the reminder of how special it is to be human,
And to be me.

Kit Birks

Silence feels kinder in the sunshine.

Burnt Toast

The man walked his dog every morning at the same easy pace, as though the world would wait for him no matter how long he took. The dog, a shaggy golden retriever with a tail that swung like a pendulum, wandered from one patch of grass to the next, nose down and ears up, fascinated by the invisible stories written in scent. Occasionally, the leash would tighten, and the man would pause, patient as a tree, waiting for the dog to finish deciphering whatever secret was tucked into a tuft of weeds or a corner of pavement.

The sun always seemed a little softer when it landed on them—a golden streak on the dog's fur, a warm splash on the man's wrinkled flannel. He would hum sometimes, low and tuneless, a sound just shy of singing, and in those moments, they were like two parts of the same quiet rhythm. They passed the same things every day: the crooked letterbox someone had painted yellow, the bench with the peeling green paint, and the old oak tree that had begun to lean over the path like it, too, wanted to listen to the hum.

But it was the little things that made the picture whole: the dog's sudden leap at a falling leaf as if it were something alive; the way the man stopped to admire a particularly bright dandelion, smiling as though he'd found treasure; the cheerful clink of the dog's tags against its collar, announcing them wherever they went. To anyone watching, it was just another walk—predictable, ordinary—but if you watched closely, you'd see the world bending toward them, as though their slowness gave everything permission to take its time.

There was a strange magic in it all, the kind you only notice if you're looking too hard or not at all. It was in the way the uneven path made their feet to fall just so, in how the clouds overhead scattered into shapes the dog might see better than the man. It was in the silence that somehow wasn't empty—filled instead with wind, with birdsong, and with the quiet communion of two beings who simply were.

And if, someday, the man walked alone—his steps slower, the leash hanging empty—you might still feel it. You'd hear the echo of tags that no longer clink, the absence of paws that no longer pounce.

But you'd know that something sacred remains: a thousand quiet walks, the golden light that always found them, and the way they slowed the world down just by being together. Love, you'd see, is not built on the grand or the loud; it's not in the big moments that make headlines or draw applause. It's in the simple, unremarkable days—where dandelions are treasures, and fallen leaves are worth chasing, and silence is a song you hum with someone who knows how to listen. It's in the way two hearts learn to move at the same unhurried rhythm, content to share nothing more than time and a stretch of earth. And even when one of them is gone, that rhythm lingers—soft and steady, like footprints pressed into the path they walked together, proof that they were here, and that the little moments were never little at all.

Burnt Toast

Life often feels like a never-ending cycle of the mundane tasks that pile up day after day.
It's dirty dishes in the sink after every meal,
Laundry baskets that fill up almost as soon as they're emptied,
Crumbs on the floor that need sweeping,
Dust settling on shelves no matter how often they're wiped,
It's the rubbish that has to be taken out,
Beds to make, shoes to put away,
Emails to answer, bills to pay,
And the endless to-do list that never seems to get shorter.

But if that's the case, then life is also....

...home-cooked meals filled with love and warmth,
It's the soft, crisp feel of clean sheets,
The smell of freshly baked bread
And the soothing sound of rain outside the window.
It's candles flickering in a cosy living room,
The satisfaction of a completed checklist,
The first sip of morning coffee,
And the stillness after tidying everything up.
It's laughter echoing through a clean home,
The glow of a sunset after a long day,
Its these small moments of peace amidst the cycle.

Life may be repetitive, but it's also rich in simple joys that make each day feel like home.

There were days when she was ready to throw in the towel on adulthood altogether,
Taxes?
Bills?
Doctor's appointments?
No, thank you,
She'd trade it all in a heartbeat for a pair of wings and a cosy life inside a tulip.

Just imagine: no emails,
Just dew drops and petal naps,
Instead of meetings,
She'd have butterfly summits,
And her toughest decision would be which flower to nap under.
Who needed a career path when you could float on the breeze,
Spreading a little sparkle and pollen?
She could croak with the frogs at passers-by,
Sunbathe all day,
And maybe even sing with the crickets at night.

How lovely to be worlds away from paying rent,
And pretending to have it all together.

Burnt Toast

It's strange that I don't know you,
The man I see walking his dog every morning,
Or the lady that shakes a tin to get her cat back inside,
Or the little boy who runs as fast as he can to the car,
Just so he can get the front seat,
And then he sticks his tongue out to his siblings,
Who ignore him,
They're clearly used to his routine,
Or the postman that whistles,
Something I used to find very annoying,
But I expect it,
So, it would be a shame if one day he decided to stop.

Or the couple that walks down the road together every single morning at 8am,
Some days holding hands,
Other days smiling and chatting,
And on the rare occasion there is distance and frostiness between them,
When this happens - I like to squint one eye and hold two fingers up to them,
And try to see if I can squish them back together,
It actually worked once and then I feared I had superpowers.
Or the gentleman who runs in the tiniest shorts imaginable,
No matter the weather – I think he is very brave,
Or the squirrel who shamelessly eats anything left on the pavement,
I saw it eat half a big mac once, I was both impressed and horrified,
Or the little birds that flit –
Wall to wall,
Tree to tree,
Wire to wire,
Singing and squawking,
I wish I knew their language.

Kit Birks

Sometimes I narrate for them,
I've created a lot of drama over the years,
One of my favourites being a twig stealing Robin,
Who caused chaos amongst the pigeons.

But oh, how I feel like I know you all,
Yet I know nothing,
No names or favourite songs,
No stories of heartbreak or what you like to eat when you're feeling low,
But,
I think that's okay,
I'm just glad that we're all here existing together,
Our lives brushing up against each other's,
In the most gentle of ways.

Burnt Toast

I love how many pockets of the universe exist—
Little corners filled with…well existing.
A farmer's market on a sleepy street,
Where sourdough is gospel, and a man named Gary
Will put up a good argument about the superiority of spelt.

Somewhere, someone's whole world
Is a knitting circle in the back of a pub,
Or a late-night radio station
Where two voices crackle like static,
Talking about nothing but meaning everything.

There's a group that meets to count stars,
Mapping constellations like they're drawing their own way home.
And another crowd stacking dominoes for hours,
Building cities out of collapse,
Only to watch it all fall with a breath.

Somewhere, a village hall fills with cake—
Victoria sponge, fruit loaves heavy with raisins,
And debates so fierce they could split kingdoms:
Jam first? Or cream?
They'll laugh about it later, but in the moment?
This is war.

There's a man who has memorised every train schedule,
Down to the minute,
And when the 4:16 pulls in exactly on time,
It makes him feel like the universe is aligned.
His joy is invisible, but it's real.

Some people march barefoot, chanting Hare Krishna,
While others march with clipboards and stopwatches,
Helping frogs cross a road they don't understand.
One cone at a time, one leap of faith.

There are dancers in basements,
Swinging to records scratched with history,
Their steps a language only they speak.
And collectors who pull joy from the air,
Chasing rare stamps or butterflies or the thrill
Of finding something no one else noticed.
And others who load their days with odd pursuits—
Like brewing mead, or hand-carving flutes,
Or debating online if a UFO's beam was real.

I love how many ways humans find
To make the world feel alive.
Like a thousand tiny fires warming a cold and endless sky.

So many people, just stumbling through pockets of the universe,
Trying to find something that feels like it's worth carrying.

Kit Birks

becoming

Burnt Toast

The thing about endings is—
we never know when they're happening.
Not really.

There was a last time my mother tucked me into bed,
but neither of us knew it.
A last time my father lifted me onto his shoulders,
before I grew too tall,
before life grew too heavy.

There was a last time my childhood dog
greeted me at the door,
tail wagging, eyes bright,
before the years slowed him down
Before the house felt emptier,

A last time my best friend and I
laughed until we couldn't breathe,
believing we had all the time in the world.

A last time I danced in the kitchen with someone I loved, before
we stopped finding reasons to stay, before goodbye settled
between us like dust.

The last time I heard my grandpa say my name,
before memory failed him,
Before time took him somewhere I could not follow
before his voice became just an echo,

We think we will remember,
that something in us will pause,
take note,
whisper 'pay attention'—

Kit Birks

But we don't mark these moments,
don't wrap them in meaning until they are gone.
Life does not warn us
when we are standing in a moment
we will ache for.

And so, we move forward,
stumbling through time,
collecting memories,
we didn't know would be our last.

Maybe that's why nostalgia feels so heavy—
not because we miss the past,
but because we never got to say goodbye to it.

Burnt Toast

It's part of being human—
to cradle the brightest joys and endure the sharpest tragedies.
It's never about choosing one or banishing the other,
but learning to let them coexist.

Joy and sorrow—
they're not enemies but reluctant roommates,
sitting side by side at the kitchen table of your heart,
each taking turns with the stories they tell.

Joy will sing of sunlit mornings
and laughter that feels eternal,
while sorrow whispers of quiet nights drenched in shadows,
where every breath feels heavier than the last.

The trick, I think,
is not to barricade them apart—
not to pretend one is more real than the other.
Instead, let them learn to lean into each other.
Let joy warm the cold hands of grief,
let grief deepen the gratitude for joy.

It's a balancing act,
a tightrope walk, over the abyss—
never knowing which will get the upper hand.
Some days, the weight of sadness will tilt the scales;
on others, happiness will rise, light as air.

But here's the secret:
when you carry them both,
when you hold that fragile equilibrium with a trembling grace,
life begins to shine in unexpected ways.

Kit Birks

The cracks in your heart catch the light like stained glass,
turning even the darkest moments into something strangely luminous.
And when you look back, you might just see it—
the beauty in the mix, the poetry in the mess.

And that is what makes life so unbearably beautiful:
Not the joy, not the tragedy,
but the way they held hands and carried you forward.
a harmony made from discord,
Creating a song, both mournful and impossibly sweet.

Burnt Toast

When we were children,
words carried a magic that seemed to shape the world around us.
"I'm sorry" was a key that unlocked forgiveness, a balm for hurt feelings.
It had a finality to it—a promise that everything was okay again.
But as adults, "I'm sorry" can lose its weight.,
It becomes a reflex, spoken out of habit or politeness,
often failing to undo the harm or repair what's broken.
We say it, knowing it may not be enough, and that realization lingers.

"Best friends forever" used to mean exactly that—
a bond unbreakable,
carved into tree trunks or scribbled in notebooks with little hearts.
As adults, we understand that friendships can fade,
not out of malice,
but because life has a way of pulling people into different currents.
"Forever", once a vow fixed in Pinky promises,
becomes conditional,
tethered to effort, proximity, and shared chapters of time.

Even the word "home" shifts.
As children, it was a fixed place,
filled with comfort, safety, and familiarity.
It was where we returned to, no matter what.
But as adults, "home" becomes elusive—
a place we have to build ourselves,
not just out of bricks and mortar,
but out of people, moments, and meaning.
And sometimes, even then, it doesn't feel quite complete.

Kit Birks

"I love you" once meant holding hands on the swings,
and fairy-tale endings,
simple, giddy, unshattered.
Now, it's layered,
complex, burdened with expectation,
A word we say with caution,
Afraid of the weight it might carry,
Or the silence it might meet,
we learn Love isn't just a feeling,
it's a choice, an action, and often, a sacrifice.
It doesn't always come with guarantees or happy endings,
and it's not always returned in the way we hope.

The innocence of childhood gives way to the intricacies of adulthood,
where words are weighed down by context, history, and unspoken emotions.
It can feel disheartening, even lonely at times,
to see the edges of words that were once magical.
How we've dulled some with overuse,
broken others in our clumsy hands.
How we've stumbled, disappointed,
 and learnt that "I'm sorry" can't always fix things,
that "forever" is a fragile promise,
and that "home" and "love" are things we must constantly redefine.

And yet, as we navigate a world far more complex than we ever imagined as children,
we slowly realise that we're all just trying our best,
that it's not about the perfect words and the perfect outcomes—
it's about effort, intention and growing from our mistakes.
All the while, still Hoping that overtime,
these once magical words might mean something again.

Burnt Toast

Sometimes we try so hard to make sense of our lives,
What it's been,
What it could be,
What it should be,
That we forget to just 'BE',
To just breathe,
Because life doesn't always need to be made sense of or planned,
It is just ours to live,
To exist in,
In any way we want it to be.

To be happy,
To be kind,
To be caring,
To love,
To get married – or don't,
To have families of our own,
To adventure, to travel, to run,
Read, relax, write, sing, paint, dance.

To take in every moment,
Like there isn't the worry of what the next minute holds,
Just this one,
Right now,
So –
Drink it in,
Quench your thirst for life by sipping each and every moment as you live it,
Experience the gift of being you,
Without any limits,
By just simply existing.

Kit Birks

When I was younger, I was the one who always tried to fix things.
A vase shattered into pieces on the floor, a shelf hanging crooked on the wall—I'd gather glue, nails, and my small hands, determined to make them whole again. I'd spend hours trying to put the shards back together or hammering a shelf into place, often working beyond reason. There were times I hurt myself in the process. My fingers bled from sharp edges of glass I couldn't quite fit, or I'd drive a nail too deep and feel the sting long after the project was done. Some of those scars have faded over time, but a few remain, pale lines tracing my younger attempts to mend what was broken.

As I grew, I realized that my need to fix things didn't stop at objects. I began to see cracks in people, fractures in their hearts and minds, and I carried the same urge to make them whole. I poured myself into their brokenness, offering every piece of me to patch their wounds, to steady their wobbling shelves of self-worth. I told myself that if I just tried harder—if I was gentler, more patient, more giving—maybe I could make them better. But I never stopped to ask what it was costing me. I didn't notice the new scars forming, deeper this time, where words cut like glass or silence hammered into me like nails. I didn't see that I was leaving pieces of myself behind in places they'd never be returned.

The truth is, I still feel like I have to fix things, even when it leaves me bleeding. And yet, I'm learning, slowly, that not everything can be mended. That maybe, the real work, is not repairing everyone else but learning to tend to my own wound. Because some cracks aren't mine to seal, and some people can't—or don't want to—be repaired. There's a heaviness that comes with letting go of that urge, a voice inside that whispers I've failed them somehow. There's a kind of grief in that realization—a mourning for the person I thought I could help them become, for the love I believed would be enough.

But it's not my responsibility to fix someone else, especially when it means leaving myself in pieces.
So, I'm learning that maybe it's okay to step back, to trust that not every broken thing needs my hands to make it whole. And that maybe the hardest and bravest thing I can do is learn that sometimes love means letting go.

When I die,
Flowers will grow from the soil where I lay planted forever,
My skin sown with the seeds of all those I have loved,
And each flower will be a person,
And each flower will be different and unique and beautiful,
They will be grown and wither and blossom again,
They will be picked and plucked and pressed between pages of old books,
They will be lovingly put behind ears of strangers,
Or placed within their hair,
Made into flower crowns,
And daisy chains,
And small bouquets – that will rest on kitchen tables,
They will bring colour and joy and scented happiness into homes,
The love they gave to me will then continue to grow,
Through multicoloured hope,
Through petals,
Through stems,
Through roots,
Through soil,
Through my skin and my bones.

Burnt Toast

It's okay to start again.
At 23, deciding to go to university
when your friends are already graduating.
At 53, stepping into a lecture hall
for the first time,
proving to yourself that it's never too late
to learn something new.

It's okay to change jobs,
to leave behind a career you thought would define you,
to chase something that feels more like you,
even if it means starting at the bottom again.
It's okay to move countries,
to pack up your life into boxes and suitcases,
to trade familiar streets for ones that don't know your name yet.

It's okay to walk away from a relationship
that no longer makes you feel alive,
even if it's been years.
It's okay to rediscover yourself,
to decide who you want to be now,
not who you were supposed to be then.

We spend so much time chasing timelines—
by 25, this.
By 30, that.
By 40, everything else.
But these deadlines are illusions,
things we made up to measure lives
that aren't meant to be compared.

There is no right time,
no finish line,
no prize for ticking off someone else's boxes.
All that matters is the life that feels good to live,
the choices that bring you closer
to who you are and what you love.

Don't chase timelines.
Chase the things that set your soul on fire.
Chase the quiet mornings that feel like peace.
Chase the dreams that keep whispering to you,
no matter how long they've waited.

Start again,
at any age,
Because you're allowed to find your happiness
as many times as it takes.
as many times as you need to.
Not because you're behind,
but because you're alive—

Burnt Toast

Maybe you're not that special.
Maybe all the feelings you hold so sacred, so uniquely yours,
are just echoes of what it means to be human.
The heartbreak that once felt like it could only belong to you,
It's etched in every love song,
whispered in every tear-soaked confession.
The joy that swells in your chest at a sunrise,
the kind that makes you feel infinite,
Someone else is watching the same sun, overwhelmed by the same quiet awe.

Your loneliness? Shared,
Your hope? Shared.
Your longing, your doubts, your fleeting moments of peace?
Shared.
Perhaps there's nothing new here,
nothing you're feeling that hasn't already been felt a thousand times,
across centuries, across lifetimes.
Maybe you're just one drop in a vast ocean of humanity,
part of something larger, but indistinct.

And yet, isn't that the miracle of it all?
To share these feelings,
to be connected by the invisible thread of simply existing?
Because no one will feel it quite like you,
 No one will turn that heartbreak into the same story,
or see that sunrise from the same angle,
at the same moment, with your exact eyes.
You are just a person, yes.
But you are this person—singular, unrepeatable, yours.
And in that, you are extraordinary.

Kit Birks

I don't think we find ourselves all at once.
It's not a sudden revelation,
Not a single moment of clarity
Where the mirror finally reflects who we are.
It happens slowly,
Like the tide pulling the shore closer,
Like sunlight stretching across a darkened room.

We find pieces of ourselves
In the quiet moments and the chaotic ones—
In the way a song can make our chest ache
Or the way a stranger's kindness
Feels like a balm on an old wound.
We learn what we love
In the things we return to over and over,
The books that fray at the edges from too many readings,
The flavours we can't resist tasting twice,
The streets that call us back
Like old friends waiting with open arms.

And we learn who we love—
Not just in the sparks of passion,
But in the soft hum of belonging,
The way their laugh feels like home,
The way their absence echoes
In places you didn't know could feel empty.

We try new things,
Some of them leaving scars,
Others leaving us breathless,
Standing on the edge of something
That feels bigger than ourselves.
The first time we climb a mountain
And see the world laid bare,
The first time we leap

Burnt Toast

Into the cold embrace of the sea
And feel the water cleanse something
We didn't know we were holding onto.

We hate this. We love that.
We make mistakes that sting for years.
We make choices that bloom into joy.
We find ourselves in the moments
Where our hearts race so fast
We forget where we are,
When the wind whips against our skin,
And for a second, we feel alive
In a way that nothing else can touch.

And it's not over—it never is.
We're not puzzles waiting to be completed,
But maps unfolding,
Revealing paths we didn't know existed.
We are the sum of everything—
Every love, every loss, every taste,
Every risk that made us tremble,
In Every quiet morning,
We chose to begin again

Imagine a world where we could see it all,
the invisible weights people carry.
A world where above every head,
A small sign hung,
Telling the truth we hide:
"I'm grieving,"
"My heart is broken,"
"My wife is sick,"
"I just lost my job,"
"I'm trapped in unkind memories."

Think of the woman who rushes past you,
her eyes fixed on the ground,
not rude but surviving,
thinking only of the hospital room
where her love lies fading.
Would you still mutter at her carelessness,
or would you offer her the kindness
she doesn't yet know how to ask for?

Picture the man at the till,
fumbling with his change,
mumbling "sorry" far too many times,
his cheeks flushed with embarrassment.
Would you see more than awkwardness?
Would you notice the weight of a redundancy letter
folded in his back pocket,
the one that reads, "We regret to inform you…"

Burnt Toast

What about the girl in the café,
staring into her coffee,
ignoring your attempt at small talk?
Would you know she's drowning in memories
that twist and bite like wolves?
That her silence isn't coldness
but survival?

If we could read the quiet truths,
the secret battles carved into every heart,
how different would the world feel?
How different would *we* be?

We might not snap so quickly.
We'd pause, breathe, and let grace lead.
We'd see not strangers, but fellow travellers
on roads just as rocky as ours.

Maybe the grumpy neighbour wouldn't seem so gruff,
the impatient driver not so cruel.
Maybe we'd realize they're not unkind by choice,
but tired from carrying more than we can see.

And slowly, the world would shift.
Each moment of understanding
like a spark in the dark,
each act of kindness
a flame passed hand to hand.

Because if only we knew,
we'd stop demanding perfection,
and start offering love.

And this is the beauty of life—
That we rise and fall, stumble and soar,
That we break and mend, then break once more,
Gathering strength in each tender scar,
Learning to love exactly as we are.

We try, we fail, then try again,
Let parts of us die, so new ones can live,
We learn to walk, to run, to rest,
Chasing calls, abandoning the rest,
We love, then lose it, cradle hearts that hurt,
Move on, keep searching, feel hope return.

We crawl through shadows, reach for light,
Breathe through the ache, surrender the fight,
And as we struggle, stumble, and yearn,
We find what it means to trust, to learn.
We laugh 'til we ache, then cry without shame,
Knowing each feeling is part of the same.

We sit in silence, we question and break,
We gather our courage with each step we take,
We walk away, then circle back,
Claim what we lost, fill what we lack.
We reach for hands that hold, then leave,
And in their absence, we learn to grieve.

We make mistakes, fall hard, then rise,
Find beauty waiting in broken skies,
We wander lost, then find the way,
Learn there's truth in what can't stay.
We let go of fear, fall apart,
And find what remains,
Is a braver heart.

Burnt Toast

This is the beauty of life unplanned—
The ache, the joy, the reach of a hand,
The falls, the climbs, the tender grace,
The endless chance to find our place.

So, for all we lose, for all we find,
We're woven deeper, soul and mind,
And every scar, and each embrace,
Leaves something timeless in our trace

Kit Birks

poems I wasn't going to include

Burnt Toast

When I was younger I found it in castles,
Ice cream, free lollipops, staying up late,
My parents tucking me in at night.

As a teenager it was kisses on the dance floor,
Posters of my favourite boy bands on my wall,
Something I thought I could have –
if I changed the way I looked

20 - I learnt it could be lost and then regained,
But each time it wouldn't look the same.

21 - That it could be used to manipulate.

23 – I saw that it could be magical, beautiful,
All consuming, painful.

24 – that sometimes it needed to be let go,
Despite all the memories,
The moments you shared,
The conversations you had late at night,
It can't be the only reason that makes you or them stay.

25 – I learnt it could blind you,
Put you in danger,
Alter your behaviour,
Break you,
Make you not want it ever again.

27 – that it's important to give it to yourself.

Kit Birks

And now,
Even after all the breaks, the bruises, the lessons, the pain,
It seems my heart won't give up,
And although as the years pass,
My understanding of it will constantly grow and change,
I'm noticing that all the love I gave away,
Is finding its way back to me.

Seeing that the right love won't manipulate,
Or put you in danger,
Or make you want to change,
That it is beautiful and magical and powerful and painful.

And ultimately that love is still found in castles,
Ice cream, lollipops, staying up late,
My parents tucking me in at night.

Burnt Toast

Excuse me…Have you seen my mind?
I've completely lost it…
Again,
It looks kind of mind shaped,
So possibly a circle or a square,
I'm not sure what colour eyes it has,
Or what style of hair.

Wait.

Hair in there?
I really hope not,
It would get too matted amongst my messy thought,
(Like a tangled ball of string that's impossible to unravel).

On second thought,
Maybe it has too much hair,
With too many strands,
Like reaching hands,
That grab onto too many things…
Too many everything's,
Too many anything's,
Too many nothing's.

That then spiral into knots,
Getting lost without a word,
Unheard by those around,
Unnoticed of how I'm starting to drown -
in the overwhelm of underwhelming thoughts.

But don't worry it will turn up,
calm down,
To repeat the same cycle –
of being lost and then re-found.

Look at you,
Flying free – out of your cocoon,
Regrown wings,
Big, bright and beautiful,
A shade of hope that really suits you,
A new you,
A true you,
A you who figured out how to reclothe themselves in strength,
After being stripped naked by your pain,
Learnt that in your darkness you weren't buried and doomed,
But rather planted so you could bloom,
Because those down days,
Are what held space,
For you to become something brand new,
To shed the layers you outgrew,
And it's okay to still have days where you sink back into the blue,
But don't think that you're regressing,
Going back a step or two,
Its just healing isn't linear,
So just remember how far you've come,
Brave, strong, beautiful, healing butterfly,
Battle scars glowing in the sun.

Burnt Toast

If you see me in full bloom,
Please do not pluck me,
And take me from a place I have longed to call home,
Leave me be
I want to stay here –
Here amongst the velvet grass,
Where the air hugs my beauty,
And my roots lay soaked in the strength of my change,
Where I have grown through the mud,
And the weeds,
And the brambles,
Waited so patiently for the sky to kiss my face,
To stand here now,
My petals unfurling,
Stretching out towards the sun,
Instead - sit here and stay with me,
Let us enjoy the light and the warmth together as one,
Even if just for a moment
Let us be proud of how far we've both come.

A special thank you to all the amazing people that helped make this book possible:

Douglas Hedges	Nancy Owen	Charles Pitts
Jeff Hill	Lanee Gray	Balázs Buczkó
Bradley Beck	Jerry Millett	Jerry Millett
Jeanette Corriell	Niall O'Sullivan	Hilmir Chadwick
Bruce Mooney	Margaret Allison	Gudmundsson
William Renner	Lynette Diaz	William Ross
Randy Jeremiah	Michelle Early	Robert Callaghan
Kim R Kee	Frank Lankford	Darren Birs
Ken Jackson	Kellene Storey	Stephan Ackermann
Nathan Albertson	John O'Rourke	Dina McShay
Doug Stewart	Julie Puglisi	Kim De La Mare
Pamela Dori-Bishop	Elisa Fetzer	Robert Chandler
Daniel Pasternack	Matt W	Yvonne Garraway
William Krafick	Philip Holmes	Laurie Lisakolsky
Kathleen Williams	Paul Nasman	Casey Mitchell
Yvonne Greer	Troy Lynette	Thomas Ferber
Dale Schorr	Jean Grubesky	Tony Negrete
Heather Rubicam	Rachel Cacciamani	Janet Warwick
Leslie Brown	William Dickey	Robert Thomson
Meaghan Kelley	Peter Greene	Petra Reimer
Gayln Snair	John Bell	Wm Kapprel
JUDY OPEL	Larry Hanson	Don Newman
Dana Kembel	Max White	Kristina Duffy
Kembel	Roy Radcliffe	Ty Gibson
Cary Greenleaf	Steven Gaconnier	Julian Veal
Margita B.Kanepaja	Andrea Bragg	Kevin Biekert
Heidi Violette	Marilyn Donaldson	Traylor McClellan
Allyson Cormier	Cheryl Hornbaker	Arnoud Schutte
Suzy Brown	Gerald Hane	Donald Lane

A special thank you to all the amazing people that helped make this book possible:

Heidi Blackmer
Paul Simpson
Mary Amabile
Ken Ringer
Chris Brain
Caroline Stone
Axel Sjøberg
Christopher Skillman
M Kruizinga
Kathleen McDonald
Drummond Johnstone
Ken Adaway
Martin Lloyd-Elliott
Raymond Wyss
Sante Boninsegna
Joe Lehrer
Dawn Manwaring
Edgardo Martir
Alexander Giorgio
David Johnson
Michael Robinson
Rachel Cacciamani
Michael Winslow
Douglas Duggan
Mark Szewczak

Robert Ledger
Michael Singer
Robert Smith
Terry Burkle
Jason Flowers
Mitch Landers
Stephan Brood
Sandra Obermeyer
Derek Lusk
Paul Adams
Gerald Grove
Justin Lovstrom
Morgan Jones
Philip Murphy
Mari Smith
Jimmy Davis
Chelsea Tidwell
Sharon McElroy
Anna Guinn
Michael Candelaria
Dana Brummett
Dennis Rooney
Gary Roth
Thomas Tymkowicz
Marilyn J Buhlmann
Amy Gui
Jason Colwell

Sharon Christian
Graham Harbord
Shelley Obrien
Krista Schwabe
David Stevenson
Anna N Rinewalt
Becky Keil
Mary Duncan
Matthew Prest
Kimberly Lorton
Scott Thieme
Christine Logsdon
Emily Pearl Campbell
Aric Allen
Christine Topping
Steve Bond
Kristina Sikes
Natalya Smirnova
Rosabella Cano
Richard Dalton
Randy Carollo
Sandi McInerney
HS de Jong
David Wahl
Jean Grubesky
Renee Peters

...try again, because everyone burns toast.

www.ingramcontent.com/pod-product-compliance
Lightning Source LLC
Chambersburg PA
CBHW060457080526
44584CB00015B/1459